SECRET MESSAGE

BIBLE
WORD SEARCHES

LARGE
PRINT

BARBOUR BOOKS

An Imprint of Barbour Publishing, Inc.

Puzzles designed by Annie Tipton, John Hudson Tiner, Kelly McIntosh, Paul Muckley, and Rebecca Germany.

ISBN 978-1-64352-030-8

All scripture quotations are taken from the King James Version of the Bible.

Published by Barbour Books, an imprint of Barbour Publishing, Inc., 1810 Barbour Drive, Uhrichsville, Ohio 44683 www.barbourbooks.com

Our mission is to inspire the world with the life-changing message of the Bible.

 Member of the
Evangelical Christian
Publishers Association

Printed in the United States of America.

WELCOME TO SECRET MESSAGE BIBLE WORD SEARCHES

If you like Bible word searches, you'll love this book. Here are dozens of puzzles to expand your Bible knowledge and test your word search skills, as many search words—each one selected from the King James Version of the Bible—await your discovery. And there's a bonus: in each puzzle the leftover letters spell out a trivia question to challenge your memory of the scripture!

Each puzzle features a scripture passage with the search words printed in **bold type**. When a phrase is **bold and underlined**, those words will be found together in the puzzle grid. Once you've found all the search words, begin at the top left-hand corner of the puzzle and read the leftover letters in order—they'll spell out the trivia question that adds to the fun. If you run into the letter "X," the question is complete. Answers—for both the puzzles and the trivia questions—begin after puzzle 49.

We know you're eager to get started, so just one final word: enjoy!

1

TROUBLE BETWEEN BROTHERS

Genesis 4:6–10

And the Lord **said unto Cain**, Why art **thou wroth**? and why is thy **countenance fallen**? If thou **doest well**, **shalt** thou not be **accepted**? and if thou doest not well, sin lieth at **the door**. And unto **thee shall** be his **desire**, and thou shalt **rule** over him. And Cain **talked** with **Abel** his brother: and it **came to pass**, **when they** were in the **field**, that Cain **rose** up **against** Abel his brother, and **slew him**. And the Lord said unto Cain, **Where** is Abel thy brother? And he said, I **know** not: **Am I my brother's keeper**? And he said, **What hast thou** done? the **voice** of thy brother's **blood crieth unto me** from **the ground**.

E E I N W H I D C E H P L A U
A C C E P T E D E M O T N U O
T S N I A G A H C K C E I D H
K L D A O L T S H A L L A R T
I E D C N V L Y M I M A C O T
S W E T A E N E L L A F T L S
B H I P H N T L W H E N H R A
L I A I E O V N E T U W E A H
O M F L P R U F U D S H G R T
O E R A T C I W I O T E R O B
D E S I R E O A R O C R O O E
T S I I L N S U R O N E U D G
D A E D K E L B R O T I N E V
E T H E Y E B N F R S H D H O
H M H W I S G A A R D E E T N

SECRET MESSAGE

_____

_____

_____

_____

_____

_____

2

SARAH'S LAUGHTER

Genesis 21:1–6

And the LORD **visited Sarah** as he had said, and the LORD did unto Sarah as he had **spoken**. For Sarah **conceived**, and **bare** Abraham a **son** in his **old age**, at the **set time** of which **God** <u>had spoken</u> to him. And **Abraham** called the **name** of his son that was **born** unto him, whom Sarah bare to him, **Isaac**. And Abraham **circumcised** his son Isaac being **eight** days old, as God had **commanded** him. And Abraham was an **hundred** years old, when his son Isaac was born unto him. And Sarah said, God <u>hath made</u> me to **laugh**, <u>so that</u> all that **hear** will laugh <u>with me</u>.

```
W H G U A L H E R C E D I S D
V H A T H M A D E O N G P W O
I D C O D M M A N N E O A I D
S D A B O R N B R C K A B T E
I E G A D L O H A E O M R H S
T M C T O D T L N I P A A M I
E I O K E I E S O V S S H E C
D T M H E A R R S E D E A A M
A C M A N D E T D D A T M H U
E N A O F M F E R N H H I M C
H A N C A A S I S A U T B U R
A R D N N T O F F E R H I N I
R G E X X M A D D V I G A B C
A E D T A H T O S A B I R I C
S O H P Q U G S D A H E R A B
```

SECRET MESSAGE

_____

_____

_____

_____

_____

3

PROMISE TO ABRAHAM

Genesis 22:15–18

And **the angel** of the L{.sc}ord **called unto Abraham** out of **heaven** the **second time**, **and said**, By **myself** have I **sworn**, saith the L{.sc}ord, for **because thou hast done this** thing, and hast not **withheld** thy son, **thine only son**: That in **blessing** I will bless thee, and in **multiplying** I will multiply **thy seed** as the **stars** of the heaven, and as the **sand** which is upon the **sea shore**; and thy seed **shall possess** the **gate** of **his enemies**; and in thy seed shall **all the nations** of the **earth** be **blessed**; because thou hast **obeyed my voice**.

E N I H T C M A H A R B A W H
O E R O H S A E S G W A L S T
T H D E M O E R L S M N S L O N
B E C A U S E A L E Y I T T H
L E I A H L T A T E C S H B O
E S O R A S T H S S D O E T A
S Y V H S H E I D A A O N L M
S H Y D T A H I P D N U A D F
E T M R N T A P M L D D T I D
D N A G E S O O Y E Y R I T N
W E E N D I B S T H N I O H E
G L O N H E O S O H L E N L V
A D A D Y N F E R T O M S G A
T I M E B L E S S I N G G I E
E O D L L A H S S W O R N D H

SECRET MESSAGE

_____

_____

_____

_____

_____

4

BABY IN AN ARK

Exodus 2:1–5

And there went **a man of** the **house of Levi**, and took to **wife** a **daughter** of Levi. And the **woman conceived**, and **bare a son**: and when **she saw him** that he was a **goodly child**, she hid him **three months**. And when she could not **longer hide** him, she took for him an **ark of bulrushes**, and **daubed** it with **slime** and **with pitch**, and put the child **therein**; and she laid it in the **flags** by the **river's brink**. And his **sister stood afar off**, to wit what would be **done to him**. And the daughter of **Pharaoh** came down to **wash herself** at the river; and her **maidens walked** along by the **river's side**; and when she saw the ark among the flags, she sent her maid **to fetch** it.

```
F N W H D A U G H T E R T S O
L A F D R E I D R E P H E H R
A M F A R I V A I O R H H E S
G O O D L Y V I V E S S T D A
S W R U G H V E E U F S E H T
P D A U B E D M R C I I O L O
T H F E L I O L S S N U W N F
S C A F H N U H B R S O P O E
L T O R T B E A R E L I C S T
I I O H A S Y A I T O O D A C
M P S O A O W M N N N U D E H
E H R W D S H A K E G T L R H
E T H E R E I N S N E D I A M
M I H O T E N O D H R B H B A
M W A L K E D F O K R A C B Y
```

SECRET MESSAGE

_____

_____

_____

_____

_____

_____

5

FOOD FROM HEAVEN

Exodus 16:2–4

And the whole **congregation** of the **children** of **Israel murmured** against **Moses** and **Aaron** in the **wilderness**: And the children of Israel **said unto** them, **Would to God** we **had died by the hand** of the Lord in the **land of Egypt**, when we sat by the **flesh pots**, and when we did **eat bread** to **the full**; for ye have **brought** us **forth** into this wilderness, to **kill this** whole **assembly** with **hunger**. Then said the Lord unto Moses, Behold, **I will rain** bread from **heaven** for you; and the **people** shall go out and **gather** a certain **rate every day**, that I may **prove** them, **whether** they **will walk** in **my law**, or no.

```
W W I L L W A L K H A T L F C
E V O R P A O M O U N T A O O
V D E R U M R U M F F H N R F
E A A S S E M B L Y A G D T O
R E H T E H W E O D R D O H S
Y R W H T D S A D E T S F S G
D B A G T H N I G H R O E P N
A T M U P I E A H E E N G E E
Y A R O S D T F H T R E Y O R
D E T R S I R T U E L A P P D
W S A B O E A N D L H L T L L
A E O N G G S L O N L T I E I
L O T N U D I A S R T H Y K H
Y E U S I W I L L R A I N B C
M H E A V E N I X T H A D A Y
```

SECRET MESSAGE

_____

_____

_____

_____

_____

6

YEAR OF LIBERTY

Leviticus 25:10–13

And ye shall **hallow** the **fiftieth year**, and **proclaim liberty throughout** all **the land** unto all the **inhabitants thereof**: it shall be **a jubile unto you**; and ye shall **return every man** unto his **possession**, and ye shall return every man unto his **family**. A jubile shall **that** fiftieth year be unto you: ye **shall not sow**, neither reap that **which groweth** of **itself** in it, **nor gather** the **grapes** in it of thy **vine undressed**. For it is **the jubile**; it shall be **holy** unto you: ye shall eat the **increase** thereof **out of the** field. In the year of **this jubile** ye shall return every man unto his possession.

```
W H A U E S A E R C N I T S H
W N O O U H T E W O R G N T C
O O D Y T U N D R E S S E D I
L I S O T H D G F A M I L Y H
L S I T E R A Y C L T T I A W
A S R N O T E T E F H H B E D
H E T U H N H B I A E R U E Y
O S D E N A L F I Y R O J E A
U S R L D E B L R L E U S F G
T O E I E N I I A O O G I L R
O P A B O I A T T H F H H E A
F F P U J V F L H A S O T S P
T H E J U B I L E E N U U T E
H M I A L C O R P H R T B I S
E V E R Y M A N I N T L S E E
```

SECRET MESSAGE

_____

_____

_____

_____

_____

7

BRAVE SPIES, FEARFUL SPIES

Numbers 13:27–30

And **they** told him, and **said**, We came unto **the land** whither **thou sentest** us, and **surely it** floweth with milk and **honey**; and this is the **fruit of it**. **Nevertheless** the **people** be **strong** that dwell in the land, and the **cities** are **walled**, and very **great**: and **moreover** we saw the **children** of Anak there. The **Amalekites dwell in** the land of the **south**: and the **Hittites**, and the **Jebusites**, and the **Amorites**, dwell in the **mountains**: and the **Canaanites** dwell by the sea, and by the coast of **Jordan**. And **Caleb stilled** the people before **Moses**, and said, **Let us go** up at once, and **possess** it; for we are well able to **overcome** it.

```
F D E L L A W L E T U S G O G
J O R D A N M O M O S E S N R
H V N O W M A A T E L P O E P
S E T I T T I H L N S R Y D A
Y R S S L Y E E D E T O I D T
H C E C E L H D T S K M U J E
S O N H A T E I S G F I E T P
N M T N R L N W R Y R B T N H
I E D E L A E E D O U Y F E U
A T V I A T A B S S I E L R S
T E T N H T E L I U T N O D E
N S A M O R I T E S O O W L I
U C R E V O E R O M F H E I T
O S S E S S O P S A I D T H I
M A N S U R E L Y I T D H C C
```

SECRET MESSAGE

_____

_____

_____

_____

_____

8

FORTY YEARS OF WANDERING

Deuteronomy 29:1–4

<u>**These are**</u> the **words** of the **covenant**, which <u>**the LORD**</u> **commanded Moses** <u>**to make**</u> with the **children** of Israel in the <u>**land of Moab**</u>, beside the covenant which <u>**he made**</u> with <u>**them in Horeb**</u>. And Moses **called** unto <u>**all Israel**</u>, and **said** unto them, Ye <u>**have seen**</u> all that the LORD did before <u>**your eyes in the land**</u> of **Egypt** unto **Pharaoh**, and unto all his **servants**, and unto all his land: the **great temptations** which thine <u>**eyes have**</u> seen, the **signs**, and those great **miracles:** Yet the LORD hath <u>**not given**</u> you an **heart** to **perceive**, and <u>**eyes to see**</u>, and <u>**ears to hear**</u>, unto this day.

```
W H E A S E R V A N T S T D I
D N D G D T N A N E V O C T S
O N R E Y N H E M A D E O N T
M O O T L P A P W D V M G E G
I T L H L L T L E I A I A R E
R G E E E A A D E K S R E D A
A I H M T A N C E H S A A L R
C V T I N A R D S T T O L I U
L E O N M E T T O W M N L H H
E N I M P L E H T F W O I C D
S H O R E B E S S E M O S I I
N C T E V A H S E Y E O R E A
S E Y E R U O Y Y V H E A D S
W T H E S E A R E I A L E B S
D E R N E P H A R A O H L S S
```

SECRET MESSAGE

_____

_____

_____

_____

_____

9

HIDDEN FROM SIGHT

Joshua 2:3–6

And the **king** of **Jericho** sent unto **Rahab, saying, Bring forth** the men that are come to thee, which are **entered** into **thine house**: for they **be come** to **search** out all the **country**. And the **woman took** the **two men**, and hid them, and **said thus**, There came **men unto** me, but I **wist not whence** they were: And it **came to pass** about the **time** of shutting of the **gate**, when it was **dark**, that the **men went out**: whither the men went **I wot not**: **pursue** after them **quickly**; for ye shall **overtake** them. But she had **brought** them up to the **roof of the house**, and **hid them** with the stalks of **flax**, which she had **laid** in **order** upon the **roof**.

S R P U R S U E N W E N I H T
S H O E A E K A T R E V O O O
A B D O T M M G E T E H N C O
P R O D F O F D A M I T D O K
O I A I W O T N O T S T H U M
T N S H O H F C B I E C O N E
E G E R A E E T W R I S U T N
M F A P I B E M H R O Y S R U
A O R S U G E E E E L U E Y N
C R C S N H T J N K H X G E T
E T H I T T O H C T A O M H O
G H Y D I A L I E L E O U G T
S A I D T H U S F R W R N S E
S H T A W Q E M I T E I E A E
M E N W E N T O U T K R A D Y

SECRET MESSAGE

_____

_____

_____

_____

_____

10

ONE GREAT SHOUT

Joshua 6:20–23

The people shouted with a **great shout**, that the **wall fell** down **flat**, so that the **people went up** into the **city, every** man **straight** before him, and they **took** the city. And they **utterly destroyed** all that was in the city, **both man** and woman, **young and old**, and **ox, and sheep**, and ass, with the **edge** of the **sword**. But **Joshua** had said unto the **two men** that had **spied out** the **country**, Go into the **harlot's house**, and **bring out** thence the **woman**, and all that she hath, as ye sware unto her. And the **young men** that were **spies** went in, and **brought** out Rahab, and her **father**, and her **mother**, and her **brethren**, and **all that she had**.

```
N W Y O U N G A N D O L D E S
A H B K X L L E F L L A W V E
M C R O N A M O W A H T S E I
H I I O G G N N P E T D S R P
T I N T N R D D H E U U R Y S
O M G U Y A A S S P O H A T E
B R O U G H T B U H D P R B D
U Y U T L A E T S E E A L R G
A T T V H B N T S E I E O E E
G T T T O E O T F G P W P T A
R S L E W L R H H A S O U H U
E L W T R O H T E R T O L R H
A O A A Y L M Y A L H H T E S
T L H E Y T Y E O S I S E N O
F R D A E Y R T N U O C L R J
```

SECRET MESSAGE

_____

_____

_____

_____

_____

11

CELESTIAL STANDSTILL

Joshua 10:11–12, 14

And it **came to pass**, as they **fled** from before **Israel**, and were in the **going** down to **Bethhoron**, that the LORD **cast down** great **stones** from **heaven** upon them unto **Azekah**, and they **died**: they were more which died with **hailstones** than they whom the **children** of Israel **slew** with the **sword**. Then **spake Joshua** to the LORD **in the day** when the LORD **delivered** up the **Amorites** before the children of Israel, and he said in the **sight** of Israel, **Sun, stand** thou **still** upon **Gibeon**; and thou, **Moon**, in the **valley of Ajalon**. . . . And there was **no day** like that **before** it or **after** it, that the LORD **hearkened** unto the **voice** of a man: for the LORD **fought** for Israel.

```
W H I B C H I L D R E N C T G
S V H D E K A I W N N G H H O
T C A E O F D I E D F G J G I
O A E L R U O V L S I A L U N
N M D I L B A R S S E M L O G
E E E V E E D S E T T H E F C
S T N E H T Y W A M N O D A Y
E O E R P H J O S H U A N A I
T P K E G H N R F A G I A E I
I A R D A O N D N A T S N U S
R S A K R R E T F A J R D E P
O S E S N O E B I G T A E C A
M Z H O I N L L I T S E L I K
A S O C A S T D O W N L F O E
R M A E I N T H E D A Y L V N
```

SECRET MESSAGE

_____

_____

_____

_____

_____

_____

12

DEADLY NAP

Judges 4:17–18, 21

Howbeit Sisera **fled away** on his **feet** to the tent of **Jael** the wife of **Heber the Kenite**: for there was **peace between Jabin** the **king** of **Hazor** and the **house** of Heber the Kenite. And Jael went out to **meet Sisera**, and **said unto** him, Turn in, **my lord**, **turn in to me**; **fear not**. And when he had **turned** in unto her into the **tent**, she **covered** him with a **mantle**. . . . Then Jael Heber's **wife** took a **nail** of the tent, and **took** an **hammer** in her **hand**, and went **softly** unto him, and **smote** the nail into **his temples**, and **fastened** it into the **ground**: for he was **fast asleep** and **weary**. **So he died**.

```
W H I S T E M P L E S T E E F
E W D N F L E D A W A Y H E J
A I E P C H E L K P R O T F A
R T N S E P T I T I H I E A B
Y T R O M E R A P N N D E S I
E S U O H O L N R E A G E T N
T D T B S E T S K H A M M E R
I R D E I T L E A J O C H N E
E O A T S T H N T T A K E E C
B L K W E T D O N N S S O D I
W Y S E R E R I A S H A Z O R
O M F E A R N O T A R M F Y T
H I B N X R X O T N U D I A S
W E D N U O R G C O V E R E D
H Y L T F O S S O H E D I E D
```

SECRET MESSAGE

_____

_____

_____

_____

_____

_____

13

THE CHOSEN ONES

Judges 7:4–5

And the LORD said unto **Gideon**, The **people** are yet **too many**; **bring** them down unto the **water**, and **I will try them for thee** there: and **it shall be**, that of **whom I say** unto thee, This shall **go with thee**, the same shall go **with thee**; and of **whomsoever** I say unto thee, This **shall not go** with thee, the same shall not go. So he **brought down** the people unto the water: and the LORD **said unto** Gideon, **Every one** that **lappeth** of the **water with his** tongue, as a **dog lappeth**, him **shalt thou set** by **himself**; **likewise** every one that **boweth down upon** his **knees** to **drink**.

```
L I K E W I S E T E S U O H T
H O N D O W N U P O N W T T M
A N I Y O I T F G K I D N H E
O O R N D L L W S N E M U E B
G B D R I L A P P E T H D R R
T G O W I T H T H E E E I E O
O L G W E R S T N S O N A L U
N E L R E Y H H A Y G P S E G
L U A P P T E F A G D U L V H
L G P P I H H S O L I T H E T
A N P W E E I W A R L D T R D
H O E H I M S E L F T B E Y O
S T T O O M A N Y E R H E O W
S I H H T I W R E T A W E N N
X X W H O M S O E V E R J E V
```

SECRET MESSAGE

_____

_____

_____

_____

_____

14

ULTIMATE SACRIFICE

Judges 11:34–36

And **Jephthah** came to **Mizpeh** unto his house, and, **behold**, his daughter came out to **meet him** with **timbrels** and with **dances**: and she was his only **child**; beside her he had **neither** son nor daughter. And it **came to pass**, when **he saw her**, that he rent his **clothes**, and said, **Alas**, my daughter! thou hast **brought** me **very low**, and **thou art one** of them that **trouble** me: for I have **opened** my **mouth** unto the LORD, and I cannot **go back**. And she said unto him, My **father**, if thou hast opened thy mouth **unto the LORD**, do to me **according** to that which hath **proceeded** out of thy mouth; **forasmuch** as the LORD hath taken **vengeance** for **thee of thine** enemies.

```
C B W N E N I H T F O E E H T
L R E M E V E R Y L O W S J H
O O H H O I E O P E N E D E O
T U P E O U T N N D I I D P U
H G R E J L T H G M E P S H A
E H O L H A D H E E T S C T R
S T C B M H C N E R A U A H T
H L E U S E E C U P M N R A O
R R E O E N E D O S Z E C H N
E R D R H I S T A R H I D E E
A U E T B G E R H W D H M S T
E R D T O M O T A I H I A E L
R E H T A F I S O R M L N D X
D A N C E S E T K C A B O G X
U N T O T H E L O R D L I H C
```

SECRET MESSAGE

_____

_____

_____

_____

_____

15

A WEDDING BANQUET

Judges 14:10–14

So his **father** <u>**went down**</u> unto the **woman**: and **Samson** made **there** a **feast**. . . . They **brought** thirty **companions** to be with him. And Samson <u>**said unto them**</u>, I will now put forth a **riddle** unto you: if ye can **certainly declare** it me **within** the <u>**seven days**</u> of the feast, and <u>**find it out**</u>, then I will give you **thirty sheets** and thirty **change** of garments: But if ye cannot declare it me, then **shall** ye <u>**give me**</u> thirty sheets and thirty change of **garments**. And they <u>**said unto him**</u>, Put **forth** thy riddle, that <u>**we may hear it**</u>. And he said unto them, Out of the **eater** <u>**came forth**</u> meat, and out of the strong came forth **sweetness**. And they **could** not in <u>**three days**</u> **expound** the riddle.

```
M E A T W H T R O F E M A C S
H S W E E T N E S S E W C R A
T H I R T Y E R E H T I E A M
E T T W O R E H T A F T R T S
G X W E N T D O W N A H T H O
A S P C I N T G E E B I A S N
R N C O H N D I M D R N I E S
M O T O U A H N A M O W N L Y
E I E D U N N R Y I U D L D A
N N I D L L D G H S G A Y D D
T A E S Y A D E E R H T S I N
S P H T R O F E A S T E T R E
E M E V I G A E R A L C E D V
N O D F F I N D I T O U T T E
O C R X M I H O T N U D I A S
```

SECRET MESSAGE

_____

_____

_____

_____

_____

16

A FOOL FOR LOVE

Judges 16:18–19

And when **Delilah** saw that he **had told** her **all his heart**, **she sent** and **called** for the **lords** of the **Philistines, saying, Come up** this once, for he **hath shewed** me all his **heart**. Then the lords of the **Philistines came** up **unto her**, and **brought money** in their **hand**. And she **made him** sleep **upon her knees**; and she **called for a man**, and she **caused** him to **shave** off the **seven locks** of his **head**; and she **began** to **afflict** him, and his **strength went from him**.

```
P W D E W E H S H T A H H O P
U H W E N T F R O M H I M N H
E A I A L S A Y I N G R A W I
M N A L S L T H E I E M S D L
O D E L I L A H R H A A E A I
C L S H L S K C O L N E V E S
M O H I I T T T E H J U N H T
I T E S D G N I T E W A A D I
H D S H Y U I G N T G V H E N
E A E E U N N S L E E P U S E
D H N A T E S O B U S A L U S
A O T R R S R O F D E L L A C
M T A T R D B R O U G H T C A
E E S N S T C I L F F A G T M
H U P O N H E R K N E E S H E
```

SECRET MESSAGE

_____

_____

_____

_____

_____

17

ONE FELL SWOOP

Judges 16:28–30

Samson called unto the LORD, and said, O **Lord GOD**, **remember** me, I pray thee, and **strengthen** me, **I pray thee**, only **this once**, O God, that **I may be** at once **avenged** of the **Philistines** for my **two eyes**. And Samson **took hold** of the two **middle pillars** upon which the **house stood**, and on which it was **borne up**, of the one with his **right hand**, and of the **other** with his **left**. And Samson said, **Let me die** with the Philistines. And he **bowed himself** with all his **might**; and the **house fell** upon the **lords**, and upon all the **people** that were **therein**. So the **dead** which he **slew** at his **death** were more than they which he slew in **his life**.

H T W H A N T T H I S O N C E
L O R D G O D F L E S M I H S
P O U E C S I D N A H L A L A
C K T S O M H I S L I F E M V
S H H D E A T H M E I T M W E
R O E E N S T R E N G T H E N
A L R T I O T H E R I G H T G
L D E L D I T O D M S A M C E
L S I O E Y N B O W E D E A D
I H N T A T E L D D I M S L E
P S F R T R M I G H T E B L S
N E P G S E Y E O W T T P E D
L I M A Y B E H D C O O M D R
H O U S E F E L L I E E F R O
O M X B O R N E U P E X Z J L

SECRET MESSAGE

_____

_____

_____

_____

_____

_____

18

RUTH'S DEDICATION

Ruth 1:16–19

And **Ruth** said, **Entreat** me not to **leave** thee, or to **return** from **following** after **thee**: for **whither** thou **goest**, I will go; and where thou **lodgest**, I will lodge: thy **people** shall be my people, and thy **God** my God: Where thou **diest**, will I die, and there will I be **buried**: the Lord do so to me, and **more** also, if **ought** but **death part** thee and me. When she saw that she was **stedfastly minded** to go with her, then she **left speaking** unto her. So they **two** went until **they came** to **Bethlehem**.

```
T F E L W H B E R E L E A V E
D I D N A O U M I A Y N D R U
L T H L I T R A P E L P O E P
V O E B E F I O R E T T H E S
Y T R R T S E I D A S T V E P
M L E D D T D O G H A H E T E
E T S E O G H E T R F E T O A
H A T H E O L U A S D E N T K
E E D D O D R F D J E U D H I
L R A E H E E X E X T G Y G N
H T K A H E T W D L S E D U G
T N S T I J U E N V R O L O G
E E I H E U R R I O B E T N L
B H U W E I N E M A C Y E H T
W M T W O N G N I W O L L O F
```

SECRET MESSAGE

_____

_____

_____

_____

_____

_____

19

A NEED MET

Ruth 2:15–19

And when she was **risen up** to glean, Boaz **commanded** his **young** men, **saying**, Let her glean even **among** the **sheaves**, and **reproach** her not: And let **fall** also some of the **handfuls** of **purpose** for her, and **leave** them, that she may **glean** them, and **rebuke** her not. **So she** gleaned in the **field** until even, and **beat** out that she had **gleaned**: and it was about an **ephah** of **barley**. And she **took** it up, and went into the **city**: and her **mother in law** saw what she had gleaned: and she **brought** forth, and gave to her that she had **reserved** after she was **sufficed**. And her mother in law said unto her, **Where hast** thou gleaned to day? and **where wroughtest thou**? **blessed** be he that did take **knowledge** of thee. And she **shewed her** mother in law **with whom** she had wrought, and said, The man's **name** with whom I wrought **to day** is **Boaz**.

```
T T O O K G L E A N E D W H A
S O T C N O R E H D E W E H S
A D S U F F I C E D U N E S L
H A O E T R E D L E I F G A U
E Y S Y V K N E P H A H D Y F
R D H I U A T D U U R U E I D
E T E B M H E M N H R O L N N
H R E M G I O H E G Y P W G A
W R O U G H T E S T T H O U H
I C O L W Y N L I A T E N S F
R R R E H E Z L C R O W M K X E
B A T L W A L N I R E H T O M
N I R X F O V B L E S S E D A
W A T A E B D E V R E S E R N
B A M O N G R E P R O A C H E
```

SECRET MESSAGE

_____

_____

_____

_____

_____

20

A VOICE IN THE NIGHT

1 Samuel 3:8–11

And the LORD called Samuel **again** the **third** time. And he **arose** and <u>**went to Eli**</u>, and said, <u>**Here am I**</u>; for thou **didst** call me. And Eli **perceived** that the LORD had called the **child**. **Therefore** <u>**Eli said**</u> unto Samuel, <u>**Go, lie down**</u>: and <u>**it shall be**</u>, if he **call thee**, that thou <u>**shalt say**</u>, Speak, LORD; for thy **servant** heareth. So Samuel went and lay down in his **place**. And the LORD **came**, and **stood**, and **called** as at **other times**, Samuel, **Samuel**. Then Samuel **answered**, **Speak**; for thy servant heareth. And the LORD said to Samuel, **Behold**, <u>**I will do**</u> a **thing** in **Israel**, at which both the **ears** of **every one** that **heareth** it shall **tingle**.

```
S E E H T L L A C B W H O W I
T E R S E E I S R A E L E T W
O H D U E H T E R A E H R E I
O I M P A R O S E I A R O E L
D A N T S O V H M F T D F L L
S H G I T S H A L L B E E D D
P C S A I S E L N M I R R I O
L R H P I R A T C T L E E A E
A O E I E N C S H I M W H S V
C L R H L A D A T A N S T I E
E A A D M D K Y C H E N D L R
G O L I E D O W N S I A G E Y
A M I L E O T T N E W N H U O
P E R C E I V E D E I T G L N
S E M I T D R I H T O S R A E
```

SECRET MESSAGE

_____

_____

_____

_____

_____

21

PROSTRATE BEFORE THE LORD

1 Samuel 5:1–4

And the **Philistines** <u>took the ark</u> of God, and brought it from **Ebenezer** unto Ashdod. When the Philistines took the **ark of God**, they **brought** it into the **house** of **Dagon**, and set it by Dagon. And when they of **Ashdod arose early** on the **morrow**, behold, Dagon was **fallen** <u>upon his face</u> to the **earth** before the <u>ark of the Lord</u>. And they **took** Dagon, and set him in his **place again**. And when <u>they arose</u> early <u>**on the morrow**</u> **morning**, **behold**, Dagon was fallen upon his face to the **ground** <u>before the ark</u> of the Lord; and the <u>**head of Dagon**</u> and both the **palms** of his **hands** were <u>**cut off**</u> upon the **threshold**; only the stump of Dagon was left to him.

```
R T D A G A I N D O D H S A B
E O N W T H R L A A A D T H E
Z O U C A H O K G R R R W O F
E K O N T H E M O R R O W U O
N R R N S M C Y N F R L S S R
E A G E R O A I A R G M E E E
B E R L E R F D O R L O T N T
E H B L A N S M H A O E D I H
T T R A R I I A P C D S R T E
K K O F T N H H U O L D E S A
M O U E H G N T T O O N A I R
N O G A D F O D A E H A R L K
T T H H E F P L A C E H L I I
S R T A F E U L I T B E Y H S
X A R K O F T H E L O R D P X
```

SECRET MESSAGE

_____

_____

_____

_____

_____

_____

22

PRACTICING FOR GOLIATH

1 Samuel 17:32–36

David said to Saul, Let no man's **heart** fail because of him; **thy servant** will **go and fight** with this **Philistine**. And Saul said to David, Thou art **not able** to go against this Philistine to fight with him: for thou **art** but a **youth**, and he a **man of war** from his youth. And David said unto Saul, Thy servant kept his father's **sheep**, and there came a **lion**, and **a bear**, and **took a lamb** out of **the flock**: And I **went out** after him, and **smote** him, and **delivered** it out of his **mouth**: and when he **arose** against me, I **caught** him by his **beard**, and smote him, and **slew him**. Thy servant slew both the lion and the bear: and this **uncircumcised** Philistine shall be as **one of them**.

```
T H Y S E R V A N T Y H O W M
H O M A E T O M S N Y O S O M
E G O A N D F I G H T O U O T
F S H K E S O R A S E T T T O
L N L E A S D M D B H A I D H
O M D E A L V A A E E I R D D
C E S T W A A E V N K A E T E
K H F H R H L M L I O N R O L
M T A B E B I R B T D F O O I
K F A S A E P M O S T E W N V
T O I T A L P A M I M U N A E
I E O T I O N A G L A I N S R
U N C I R C U M C I S E D T E
G O O L I C A U G H T R A A D
T W E N T O U T H P B E A R D
```

SECRET MESSAGE

_____

_____

_____

_____

_____

23

A GIANT CHALLENGE

1 Samuel 17:43, 46, 49–51

And the **Philistine said** unto **David**, <u>**Am I a dog**</u>, that thou **comest** to me with **staves**? And the Philistine **cursed** David by <u>**his gods**</u>. . . . <u>**This day**</u> will the LORD **deliver** thee into <u>**mine hand**</u>; and I will **smite** thee. . . . David put <u>**his hand**</u> in <u>**his bag**</u>, and **took thence** a stone, and **slang** it, and smote the Philistine in his **forehead**, that the stone <u>**sunk into**</u> his forehead; and he <u>**fell upon**</u> <u>**his face**</u> to the **earth**. So David **prevailed** over the Philistine with a **sling** and with a **stone**, and **smote** the Philistine, and <u>**slew him**</u>; but there was no **sword** in the <u>**hand of David**</u>. . . . When the Philistines saw their **champion** was **dead**, <u>**they fled**</u>.

```
E C N E H T S U N K I N T O N
C O H D R O W S W H L D E O R
A M G A E W E H A S I O P T D
F E N H M V E A P V L U R A A
S S A C A P E N A I L S A D E
I T L T S A I D S L R M M N H
H I S B A G D O E A E O I M E
D L T L F A A F N S C T A I R
E D O E E D T D H M S E D N O
L N N D H W E A E I S P O E F
F A E H T S H V L T I L G H L
Y H I S R E V I L E D T I A I
E S N U A E H D M K O O T N S
H I C X E P R E V A I L E D G
T H I S D A Y X S D O G S I H
```

SECRET MESSAGE

_____

_____

_____

_____

_____

DAVID THE MAD MAN

1 Samuel 21:10–15

And **David** arose and **fled** that day for fear of **Saul**, and went to **Achish** the **king of Gath**. And the **servants** of Achish said unto him, Is not this David the king of the **land**? did they not **sing** one to another of him in **dances, saying**, Saul hath **slain** his **thousands**, and David his ten thousands? And David laid up these words in his **heart**, and was **sore afraid** of Achish the king of Gath. And he **changed** his **behaviour** before them, and **feigned** himself mad in their hands, and **scrabbled** on the **doors** of the **gate**, and let his **spittle** fall down upon his **beard**. Then said Achish unto his servants, **Lo, ye see** the man is mad: **wherefore** then have ye **brought** him to me? **Have I need** of **mad men**?

```
W B H A T K D O O R S E W A D
S T R S C H I E L T T N N E A
M S E O O H O N R A E F N T H
F L E D U R A A G M N G E C R
A L R R V G E N D O I D E T U
S A O H V H H A G E F A T D O
A C F Y A A M T F E V G I D I
Y H E E E D N S C R D A A P V
I I R E D S A T T O A R A T A
N S E F T L E V S S E I A R H
G H H H H A V E I N E E D E E
I N W S P I E R I D O C D W B
I T I S D N A S U O H T N H K
I N G S C R A B B L E D A A C
E L T T I P S A U L H I S H D
```

SECRET MESSAGE

_____

_____

_____

_____

_____

25

CAN'T TOUCH THIS

2 Samuel 6:5–9

And **David** and all the **house** of **Israel played** before the LORD on all **manner** of **instruments** made of fir **wood**, even on **harps**, and on **psalteries**, and on **timbrels**, and on **cornets**, and on **cymbals**. And when they came to **Nachon's threshingfloor**, **Uzzah** put forth his hand to the <u>**ark of God**</u>, and <u>**took hold**</u> of it; for the **oxen shook** it. And the **anger** of the LORD was **kindled** against Uzzah; and God **smote** him there for his **error**; and there he **died** by the ark of God. And David was **displeased**, **because** the LORD had made a **breach** upon Uzzah: and he **called** the **name** of the **place Perezuzzah** to <u>**this day**</u>. And David was **afraid** of the LORD that day.

```
A T W S H D O T O O K H O L D
N S H P C E I L H S E D R O L
G T H R M Y E S E I I O B X H
E I U A E A M I P A S S E E C
R M N H R S R B R L H D C N A
D B D S E E H F A A E A A H E
E R I E T L A I Z L L A U Y R
Y E V L D R S Z N P S D S D B
A L A T E N U D H G E E E E A
L S D N O Z Z M E R F L K F D
P O N H E R Z T E I D L H K R
R A C R D E A E M N D A O O O
M A E S U O H O I N T C T O R
N P D O G F O K R A H S S H R
S T E N R O C W X E T O M S E
```

SECRET MESSAGE

_____

_____

_____

_____

_____

26

DANCING IN THE STREETS

2 Samuel 6:14–17

And **David danced** before the Lord with all his **might**; and David was **girded** with a **linen ephod**. So David and all the <u>**house of Israel**</u> brought up the <u>**ark of the Lord**</u> with shouting, and with the **sound** of the **trumpet**. And as the ark of the Lord **came** into the <u>**city of David**</u>, **Michal** Saul's **daughter looked through** a **window**, and saw **king** David **leaping** and **dancing** <u>**before the Lord**</u>; and she despised him in her **heart**. And they **brought** in the ark of the Lord, and set it in his **place**, in the **midst** of the **tabernacle** that David had **pitched** for it: and David **offered burnt offerings** and **peace** offerings **before** the Lord.

```
D W H D I V A D F O Y T I C C
L A H C I M E T R U M P E T A
A T U R E K D T H R O U G H M
S S U G O E R O F E B L N G E
E G T O H L O R D E D F I I C
L N L R O T L M P M I C P M A
C I H O U S E O F I S R A E L
A R N E H A H R E D T D E D P
N E L E P G T D N C I C L E S
R F B A N H F U A V A D H R D
E F B I G A O D A N C E D E E
B O K U T S K D T I C T P F D
A U O D R E R W O D N I W F R
T R A E H N A T S D I M N O I
B E F O R E T H E L O R D G G
```

SECRET MESSAGE

_____

_____

_____

_____

_____

27

TEMPTING VISION

2 Samuel 11:2–6

And it came to pass in an **eveningtide**, that **David arose** from **off his bed**, and **walked** <u>**upon the roof**</u> of the <u>**king's house**</u>: and from the **roof** he saw a woman **washing herself**; and the woman was very **beautiful** to **look** upon. And David sent and **enquired** after the woman. And <u>**one said**</u>, Is not this **Bathsheba**, the **daughter** of **Eliam**, the **wife** of **Uriah** the **Hittite**? And David sent **messengers**, and **took** her; and she came in unto him, and he <u>**lay with her**</u>; for she was **purified** from her **uncleanness**: and she **returned** unto her **house**. And the **woman conceived**, and sent and **told** David, and said, I am with **child**. And David sent to **Joab**, saying, Send me Uriah the Hittite.

```
U N C L E A N N E S S E F I W
P W H A T P U R I F I E D A R
O E L I A M D E N R U T E R D
N D N A M O W U D M Y I E L K
T E I L Y L F I R E E T O E A
H R D D U W V F S I H T D B E
E I E H R A I U H G A I E S S
R U V E D S O T U I T H O C U
O Q I R B H I A H G S R A H O
O N E S A I D H N H A B K I H
F E C E O N D I T U E O E L S
R I N L J G N A F O O R N D G
G A O F B E B W A L K E D A N
T T C L V L U F I T U A E B I
E S R E G N E S S E M T O O K
```

SECRET MESSAGE

_____

_____

_____

_____

_____

BATTLING OTHER GIANTS

2 Samuel 21:19–21

And there was again a **battle** in **Gob** with the **Philistines**, where **Elhanan** the son of **Jaareoregim**, a **Bethlehemite**, slew the **brother** of **Goliath** the Gittite, the **staff** of whose **spear** was like a **weaver's beam**. And there was yet a battle in **Gath**, where was a man of **great stature**, that had on **every hand** six **fingers**, and on every **foot six toes**, **four and twenty** in **number**; and he also was born to the **giant**. And when he **defied Israel, Jonathan** the son of **Shimeah** the brother of **David slew him**.

```
S S S W J O N A T H A N S H W
P H I L I S T I N E S R A T E
E I G D E B R O T H E R I G A
A M A E N W E N T G I C K E V
R E I F N A H L N J O G H R E
D A V I D A H I H A D B A U R
N H I E S R F Y M A O N G T S
B E D D T R R H R R N A I A B
F F A T S E A T W E A A A T E
S O V F B E E E R O V T N S A
H I O M R T O E L R E E T T M
F O U R A N D T W E N T Y A N
T N B A T T L E X G A T H E F
B E T H L E H E M I T E E R E
T H T A I L O G L M S O N G G
```

SECRET MESSAGE

_____

_____

_____

_____

_____

29

SOLOMON'S WISE REQUEST

1 Kings 3:11–14

Because thou hast asked this **thing**, and hast not **asked** for thyself <u>**long life**</u>; neither hast asked **riches** for thyself, nor hast asked the **life** of thine enemies; but hast asked for thyself understanding to **discern judgment**; **behold**, I have done **according** to thy **words**: lo, I have **given** thee a **wise** and an understanding **heart**; so that there was none like thee before thee, **neither** after thee shall any **arise** like unto thee. And I have also given thee that which thou hast not asked, both riches, and **honour**: so that there shall not be any among the **kings** like unto thee <u>**all thy days**</u>. And if thou <u>**wilt walk**</u> in my **ways**, to **keep** my **statutes** and my **commandments**. . .then I will **lengthen** thy days.

```
W C H I C H Q S E T U T A T S
D O L O N G L I F E D U E Y Y
I M E N W T T R A V L E A L A
S M E D I T H O J E O W R R D
C A K U S S I A L T H S I E Y
E N M I E T N O N S E E S E H
R D E S N O G E L H B O E M T
N M O H N G M S C W I S D O L
K E E P T G S I M W O R D S L
F N I R D G R U O N O H S G A
D T T U H A N N D T X X F I A
E S J P L N T E R L O N L V Y
K O W I L T W A L K H E A E A
S L F O M N E I T H E R S N D
A E E E R H A C C O R D I N G
```

SECRET MESSAGE

_____

_____

_____

_____

_____

30

THE HOUSE OF THE LORD

1 Kings 7:48–51

And **Solomon** made all the **vessels** that pertained unto the **house** of the LORD: the **altar** of gold, and the **table** of **gold**, whereupon the **shewbread** was, and the **candlesticks** of **pure** gold, **five** on the **right** side, and five on the **left**, before the **oracle**, with the **flowers**, and the **lamps**, and the **tongs** of gold, and the **bowls**, and the **snuffers**, and the **basons**, and the **spoons**, and the **censers** of pure gold; and the **hinges** of gold, both for the **doors** of the **inner** house, the most **holy** place, and for the doors of the house, to **wit**, of the **temple**. So was **ended** all the **work** that **king** Solomon **made** for the house of the LORD.

```
H O W C E N S E R S E G N I H
D M A N Y Y F E A R S T O T A
L O H D I S I E D I T S T G A R
R K O E S H V L O L K O O S O
I M L R O E E B N C T L P O S
G B Y U S W I A I L D O D L T
H H I S S B O T W K O M W N F
T P E E R R S S I N H O U S E
O L N A E E L N S H B N P E L
S R A T L A G O U M E I U L A
L O R D C D X S X F I N R P M
R I N M A P G W I T F N E M P
I A A F R N E N D E D E R E S
C D F L O W E R S N E R R T O
E S L T W O R K B A S O N S W
```

SECRET MESSAGE

_____

_____

_____

_____

_____

31

SOLOMON AND SHEBA

1 Kings 10:4–8

And when the **queen** of **Sheba** had seen all **Solomon's** wisdom, and the house that he had **built**, and the meat of his **table**, and the **sitting** of his **servants**, and the **attendance** of his **ministers**, and their **apparel**, and his **cupbearers**, and his **ascent** by which he went up unto the **house of the LORD**; there was no more **spirit** in her. And she said to the king, It was a **true report** that I heard in mine **own land** of thy acts and of thy wisdom. **Howbeit** I **believed** not the **words**, until I came, and **mine eyes** had seen it: and, behold, **the half was not told me**: thy wisdom and **prosperity exceedeth** the fame which I heard. **Happy** are thy men, happy are these thy servants, which **stand continually** before thee, and **that hear thy wisdom**.

```
H O W M O D S I W Y H T D I D
H A P P A R E L D N A T S T H
A E Q S N O M O L O S U R E T
P B C E T L E X C E E D E T H
P B E O O E F L A H E H T P A
Y U E H N H C N B C O R S R T
Q I D F S T S N U A O H I O H
M L E E A F I P A P T T N S E
I T V S W O B N E D I B I P A
N A E P A E W R U E N T M E R
E T I I A S E N B A T E M R E
E S L R T U C W L I L D T I S
Y O E I R O O E N A L L L T O
E R B T M H O G N O N N Y Y A
S E R V A N T S T T S D R O W
```

SECRET MESSAGE

_____

_____

_____

_____

_____

32

VOICE OF GOD

1 Kings 19:10–12

And he said, I have been very **jealous** for the L<small>ORD</small> **God** of **hosts**: for the **children** of **Israel** have **for-saken** thy **covenant, thrown** down **thine altars**, and **slain** thy **prophets** with the sword; and I, **even I only, am left**; and they **seek my life**, to take **it away**. And he said, Go **forth**, and **stand** upon the mount before the L<small>ORD</small>. And, behold, the L<small>ORD</small> **passed** by, and a **great** and **strong wind rent** the **mountains**, and **brake** in pieces the **rocks** before the L<small>ORD</small>; but the L<small>ORD</small> was **not in the wind**: and after the wind an **earthquake**; but the L<small>ORD</small> was not in the earthquake: and after the earthquake **a fire**; but the L<small>ORD</small> was not **in the fire**: and after the fire a **still small voice**.

```
W N O T I N T H E W I N D H E
G T N A N E V O C L R E O E Y
R O C K S M Y L I F E K G P A
E E E S T E H P O R P A D A W
A W V N W S A S V E L R R S A
T L I E I J N A L H E B O S T
H I T K N H I I L K D I L E I
N N G A D I T W A H S C E D N
T T H S R E O U M T H W O R J
D H E R E S Q N S I N O F E N
T E R O N H H O L F S U A W S
K F I F T E H D L Y O L O T L
O I F R R D R C I A O R A M M
E R A M L E F T T U H N T I T
O E H G N O R T S T D I M H N
```

SECRET MESSAGE

_____

_____

_____

_____

_____

33

THE CAPTAIN AND THE SLAVE GIRL

2 Kings 5:1–4

Now Naaman, **captain** of the **host** of the **king** of Syria, was a **great** man with his **master**, and **honourable**, **because** by him the LORD had **given deliverance** unto Syria: he was also a **mighty** man in **valour**, but he was a **leper**. And the **Syrians** had gone out by **companies**, and had **brought away captive** out of the **land** of Israel a <u>little maid</u>; and she **waited** on Naaman's **wife**. And she said unto her **mistress**, **Would** God my lord **were** with the **prophet** that is in **Samaria**! for he would **recover** him of his **leprosy**. And <u>one went</u> in, and told his lord, **saying**, <u>Thus and</u> thus said the maid that is of the land **of Israel**.

```
D W H Y O P S E M E S S E N G
L E M E S R E P E L R H T O L
U V L I D O T H G U O R B N A
O I C I G P R A S N A I R Y S
W T O R V H M P O V A L O U R
R P M D E E T U E I E A O A N
E A P I I T R Y R L S N D R A
C C A T S A S A E O U D N W D
O G N W B T M A N A A M A N S
V N I L A A R E M C C Y S S H
E I E I S S G E L N E N U T H
R Y S W I R H O S T B E H W K
E A J F E R E W O S T V T I R
D S O A A N C A P T A I N F N
R I T V D E T I A W E G L E R
```

SECRET MESSAGE

_____

_____

_____

_____

_____

34

A Leper Healed

2 Kings 5:13–15

And his **servants** came **near**, and **spake** unto him, and said, My **father**, if the **prophet** had **bid** thee do some **great thing**, wouldest thou not have done it? how much **rather** then, when he **saith** to thee, **Wash**, and be **clean**? Then went he **down**, and **dipped** himself <u>**seven times**</u> in **Jordan**, according to the **saying** of the <u>**man of God**</u>: and his **flesh** came **again** like unto the flesh of a **little child**, and he was clean. And he **returned** to the man of God, he and all his **company**, and **came**, and **stood before** him: and he said, **Behold**, now I **know** that there is no God in all the **earth**, but in **Israel**: now therefore, I **pray** thee, take a **blessing** of thy servant.

```
N L I T T L E R E H T A R B R
S E V E N T I M E S W H A E T
Y N A P M O C W A S T H T F E
T A E R G B E H O L D U D O L
E G N I Y A S N A D R O J R P
E A R N S T O O D N G A A E M
A I E K A P S N E F H T R A E
D N P S I P T D O C A M E O S
E I R T T I N N O N U K N O W
P N A D H E A R T H T E W K I
P N Y G O M V F T E H P O R P
I S Y L E A R S I R I I D A H
D L I H C L E A N X N X O A S
I D E B L E S S I N G L J F A
B E L F H S E L F A T H E R W
```

SECRET MESSAGE

_____

_____

_____

_____

_____

35

THE MISSING ENEMY

2 Kings 7:5–7

And they **rose up** in the **twilight**, to go unto the camp of the **Syrians**: and **when** they were **come** to the **uttermost part** of the **camp of Syria**, **behold**, there was **no man there**. For the LORD had **made** the host of the Syrians to **hear** a **noise** of **chariots**, and a noise of **horses**, **even** the noise of a **great host**: and they said one to **another**, Lo, the **king of Israel** hath **hired against** us the **kings** of the **Hittites**, and the kings of the **Egyptians**, to come upon us. **Wherefore they arose and fled** in the twilight, and **left their tents**, and their horses, and their asses, even the camp as it was, and **fled for their life**.

```
W H K I N G S O R O F D E L F
K T F I L O R D R S C T E E P
D I R T S N I A G A R F V U I
S S N A I R Y S M A T E E T C
O D S G P H V P E T N S S H E
R L E E O D O H H A O O N E T
W O T R T F H E N R M R A I A
T H S S S I I O T R A A I R H
E E Y O R T S E S N Y T L A
S B R N T H D T R Y T E P I N
E I R E E E T M I A H H Y F D
A M N R R U I A A H E T G E F
S T O I R A H C E D R L E A L
S N H C S H W H E R E F O R E
A D F L E T W I L I G H T D D
```

SECRET MESSAGE

_____

_____

_____

_____

_____

36

DAVID'S THREE MIGHTIEST MEN

1 Chronicles 11:17–19

David longed, and said, Oh that one would **give** me **drink** of the water of the well of **Bethlehem**, that is at **the gate**! And the **three brake** through the **host** of the **Philistines**, and **drew water** out of the well of Bethlehem, that was by the gate, and **took it**, and **brought** it to David: but David would not drink of it, but **poured** it out to the LORD. And said, **My God forbid** it me, that I **should do this thing**: shall I drink the **blood** of these men that have put their **lives** in **jeopardy**? for with the jeopardy of their lives they brought it. **Therefore** he would not drink it. These things did these three **mightiest**.

```
T O O K I T H I S T H I N G A
M F P T J E R B T H E T H I R
E Y E H M E I D R I N K G V L
H T G I I D O E E A S T H E O
O B W O I L T P M P K A N Y R
S L E B D A I O A O O E L D D
I O R T W E R S D R S U W T I
E O R W H E B D T P D A R H V
F D E R T L L R O I F Y K E A
I R H N G U E O O D N A V G D
D I D O O S N H N U S E E A X
T G R H S O U P E G G E S T O
F T S E I T H G I M E H V E E
T H R E E L I T E W A D T I R
R I O T H E R E F O R E R S L
```

SECRET MESSAGE

_____

_____

_____

_____

_____

_____

37

GETTING READY TO BUILD

1 Chronicles 22:14–16

Now, behold, in my **trouble** <u>**I have**</u> **prepared** <u>**for the**</u> **house** of the LORD an **hundred thousand talents** <u>**of**</u> <u>**gold**</u>, and a thousand thousand talents **of silver**; and of **brass** <u>**and iron**</u> without **weight**; for it is in **abundance**: timber also and stone have I prepared; and thou mayest add thereto. **Moreover** <u>**there are**</u> **workmen** with thee in abundance, **hewers** and **workers** <u>**of**</u> <u>**stone**</u> <u>**and timber**</u>, and all <u>**manner of**</u> **cunning** <u>**men**</u> <u>**for**</u> **every** manner of work. Of the gold, the silver, and the brass, and the iron, there **is** <u>**no**</u> **number**. **Arise therefore**, <u>**and be**</u> **doing**, and the LORD **be with thee**.

```
E B D N A W H P Y F G N I O D
S S A R B W M O R E O V E R R
U E R A E R E H T E N R O A O
O T R O U B L E S O P L T D F
H S A B V I M D R N D A O H N
T A R L E L R I O W E B R C E
E D E E T W D E T O R U U E M
E B V U K N I H B D D N I V D
O S L T A R E T N M N D W A L
F L I I A R O A H I U A O H O
S D S R E L S W N T H N R I G
T N F F A U E G A H H C K O F
O U O F O R E N N A M E M S O
N R T H G I E W T E E V E R Y
E F T O H E W E R S R G N O D
```

SECRET MESSAGE

_____

_____

_____

_____

_____

_____

38

PROMISE OF HEALING

2 Chronicles 7:14–16

If **my people**, **which** are **called** by **my name**, **shall humble themselves**, **and pray**, **and seek my face**, and **turn from** their **wicked ways**; **then will I hear** from **heaven**, and will **forgive their sin**, and **will heal their land**. Now **mine eyes** shall be **open**, and mine **ears attent unto** the **prayer** that is **made** in this **place**. For now have I **chosen** and **sanctified** this **house**, that my name may be there for ever: and mine eyes and mine **heart** shall **be there perpetually**.

```
P R A Y E R W H O B D N E H T
U E I F O R G I V E H L L O T
Y A R P D N A T I U H L P E T
H P O P O U S F M C L E O H E
T H L T E A I B T A N S E Y E
G M N A H T L O H L E M P W N
E U Y I C E U S W L S A Y I E
A D K N S E I A I E O D M C V
R T A E A R H R L D H E A K A
S S T R E M I V L L C F A E E
E D C E W S E E I A Y S H D H
S O S H N S D E H M N E Y N T
U O I T S T A N E T N D N A C
O C H E A R T L A E H L L I W
H T I B F Y T U R N F R O M M
```

SECRET MESSAGE

_____

_____

_____

_____

_____

_____

39

HAND OF GOD

Ezra 8:21–23

Then I **proclaimed** a fast there, at the **river** of **Ahava**, that we might **afflict ourselves before** our God, to seek of him a **right** way for us, and for our <u>**little ones**</u>, and for all our **substance**. For I was **ashamed** to **require** of the <u>**king a band**</u> of **soldiers** and **horsemen** to help us against the **enemy** in the way: **because** we had **spoken** unto the king, **saying**, <u>**The hand of our God is upon all them for good that seek him**</u>; but his **power** and his **wrath** is against all them that **forsake** him. So we **fasted** and **besought** our God for this: and he was **intreated** of us.

L K W D O G R U O F O H E A D
M I H K E E S T A H T R E F E
W N T N E M E S R O H H S F T
A G N T E S I E D Z R P G L A
A A O G L N R A O N O I O I E
B B P N G E E F L K A U W C R
E A U H Q S O M E C R H N T T
F N S U U R E N Y S O A E T N
O D I A S H A M E D T R E H I
R R C A T V W L N S H E P G T
E E K L A R V A B S K E D U F
B E L H A E O U F O R G O O D
R A A T S V S O L D I E R S A
S A H G N I Y A S F A S T E D
F E J O U R E W O P R N E B Y

SECRET MESSAGE

_____

_____

_____

_____

_____

_____

40

CITY IN RUINS

Nehemiah 2:2–5

Wherefore the **king said** unto me, Why is thy **countenance** sad, seeing thou **art not sick**? this is **nothing** else but **sorrow of heart**. Then I was very sore **afraid**, and said unto the king, Let the **king live** for ever: why should not my countenance **be sad**, when **the city**, the place of my **fathers' sepulchres**, lieth **waste**, and the **gates thereof** are **consumed with fire**? Then the king said unto me, For what dost thou make **request**? So I **prayed** to the **God of heaven**. And I said unto the king, If it **please** the king, and if thy **servant** have **found favour** in **thy sight**, that thou **wouldest** send me unto **Judah**, unto the **city of my** fathers' sepulchres, that I **may build it**.

```
E T S A W W W I T H F I R E A N
N S H H F A S O R R O W O F F
T E P T E A O S T S E U Q E R
T D V C H A T D I A R D N E A
H L E A O G R H R M E I A H I
D U M H E U I T E N H A Y S D
I O A F V H N S O R T S M E E
A W Y W A O F T Y B S E F P I
S T B D T V H O E H E R O U H
G K U S F I O S D N T V Y L I
N J I N N O A U G O A A T C A
I C L G R D U T R A G N I H X
K E D E M U S N O C R T C R X
E V I L G N I K D P R A Y E D
E S T H E C I T Y P L E A S E
```

SECRET MESSAGE

_____

_____

_____

_____

_____

41

COURAGEOUS QUEEN

Esther 4:14–16

For if thou **altogether holdest** thy **peace** at **this time**, then **shall** there **enlargement** and **deliverance arise** to the Jews from **another place**; but thou and thy **father's house** shall be **destroyed**: and who **knoweth whether** thou art come to the **kingdom** for such a time as this? Then **Esther** bade them **return Mordecai** this **answer**, Go, **gather** together all the Jews that are **present** in **Shushan**, and **fast ye for** me, and **neither eat nor drink three days, night** or day: I also and my **maidens** will fast **likewise**; and so will I go in unto the king, which is not **according** to the law: and if I perish, **I perish**.

```
A D K N O W E T H H O W W W A
D N E N R E S U O H S E H S H
E T S L I U E H F A T H E R S
S P I W I R T R U H E A T E I
T R W R E V D E H S L E H H R
R E E R E R E R R T H C E T E
O S K G N I D R O C C A R O P
Y E I L A T E G A N D E N N I
E N L A R G E M E N T P G A T
D T H I S T I M E T C A C S H
A O R E H T I E N M T E E H G
R O F E Y T S A F H D D C A I
I O R E H T S E E R L A A L N
S N E D I A M R O O R Y L L D
E K I N G D O M H E C S P A I
```

SECRET MESSAGE

_____

_____

_____

_____

_____

42

ESTHER APPROACHES THE KING

Esther 7:1–4

So the **king** and **Haman** came to **banquet** with **Esther** the **queen**. And the king said again unto Esther on the **second day** at the banquet of **wine**, What is thy **petition**, queen Esther? and it shall be **granted** thee: and what is thy **request**? and it shall be **performed**, even to the **half** of the **kingdom**. Then Esther the queen **answered** and said, If I have found **favour** in thy **sight**, O king, and if it **please** the king, let my **life** be **given** me at my petition, and my **people** at my request: For we are **sold**, I and my people, to be **destroyed**, to be **slain**, and to **perish**. But if we had been sold for **bondmen** and **bondwomen**, I had held my **tongue**, although the **enemy** could not countervail the king's **damage**.

```
W H A A N S W E R E D T P N P
P E T I T I O N E R S E O E E
T E U Q N A B E F I L S N E R
A B O N D W O M E N L A P U F
D N O C E S O Y S I S E D Q O
E A S F S V I O G A N L E R R
D M L I D K I I N L O P T E M
N A G A H A S G I S U E N Q E
H H M O D G N I K R U S A U D
S G R E H T S E P I V E R E T
I E D E Y O R T S E D U G S T
R O N B O N D M E N O M O T H
E R D I E G C A I V Y P X X G
P H A M W U L I A S A C L A I
D A M A G E A F O T D R D R E S
```

SECRET MESSAGE

_____

_____

_____

_____

_____

43

JOB IS BLESSED

Job 42:12–16

So the LORD **blessed** the **latter end** of **Job** more than his **beginning**: for he had **fourteen** thousand **sheep**, and **six** thousand **camels**, and a **thousand yoke** of **oxen**, and a thousand she **asses**. He had also **seven sons** and **three daughters**. And he **called** the **name** of the first, **Jemima**; and the name of the second, **Kezia**; and the name of the third, Kerenhappuch. And in **all** the **land** were no **women found** so **fair** as the daughters of Job: and their **father** gave them inheritance among their brethren. After this lived Job an hundred and **forty years**, and **saw** his sons, and his sons' sons, even **four** generations.

```
J E M I M A W H A T D S I D F
Y S A T S A W A N C L L A D O
S E S S A I M O W E O D U A R
D L A D I J O B M B E N J U T
E O B R S X N A R E E U S G Y
L P D O S E C N S E N O I H F
L T N H V E L O R I A F R T D
A T A E E R H T O O K O X E N
C E S V D E R F D L Y U T R P
H I U R N N O E E A A R G S E
Y F O R E U M O S I M T H I E
O L H M R A X X S Z A E T J H
K J T S N O S A E E L E S E S
E L O A C D N A L K L N K A R
G N I N N I G E B F A T H E R
```

SECRET MESSAGE

_____

_____

_____

_____

_____

44

ROOTED IN RIGHTEOUSNESS

Psalm 1:1–5

Blessed is the man that **walketh** not in the **counsel** of the **ungodly**, nor **standeth** in the way of **sinners**, nor **sitteth** in the **seat** of the **scornful**. But his **delight** is in the law of the LORD; and in his law doth he **meditate** day and **night**. And he **shall** be like a **tree planted** by the **rivers** of **water**, that **bringeth forth** his **fruit** in his **season**; his **leaf** also shall not **wither**; and **whatsoever** he doeth shall **prosper**. The ungodly are not so: but are like the **chaff** which the **wind driveth away**. **Therefore** the ungodly shall not stand in the **judgment**, nor sinners in the **congregation** of the **righteous**.

```
S C W B R I N G E T H H A T D
C O N G R E G A T I O N H O E
O U I C W S V H P L A N T E D
R N G H H I E E W I T H E R T
N S H A T R N S O H L I K S P
F E T F E E I D E S S E L B S
U L N F V T T G A A T A A L M
L S O A I A R T H Y T A W F S
S R S H R T E T I T A P H A L
E R A L D I E H A S E R L W Y
T N E M G D U J U N G O D L Y
I P S N N E R I V E R S U P E
U N T A N M O T H D E P U S N
R G T H G I L E D O R E T A W
F S L L A H S D L H T R O F Y
```

SECRET MESSAGE

_____

_____

_____

_____

_____

45

DESPAIR

Psalm 22:1–6

My God, my God, why hast thou **forsaken me**? why art **thou so** far from **helping me**, and from the **words** of my **roaring**? O my God, **I cry in** the day **time**, but thou **hearest** not; and in the **night season**, and **am not** silent. But thou **art holy**, O thou that **inhabitest** the **praises** of Israel. Our **fathers trusted in thee**: they trusted, and **thou didst** deliver them. They **cried unto thee**, and were **delivered**: they trusted in thee, and **were not confounded**. But **I am a worm**, and no man; a **reproach** of men, and **despised** of the **people**.

```
W F A T H E R S H O I N T H E
T H O U D I D S T N E T W S T
E D E R E V I L E D H S I I S
R T E A S S E A S O N L N N D
O M M I Y A E N U T E T I T R
A U G R R L K S S N C D Y H O
R S N A O C O E T O N E R E W
I E I T I W T H N D T T C E H
N E P O O I A F T M H S I P E
G N L R B T O M Y R E U I P L
T N E A O U H G A S A R G E W
H I H N N A O E I I R T A O O
G N M D R D C A E D E R S P O
I A E E F T R H H I S S P L S
N D E S I P S E D I T A L E M
```

SECRET MESSAGE

_____

_____

_____

_____

_____

_____

46

PRAISE THE LORD!

Psalm 95:3–9

For the LORD is a **great God**, and a **great King above all** gods. In his **hand are** the deep **places** of the **earth**: the **strength** of the **hills** is his also. The **sea is his**, and **he made it**: and his **hands formed** the **dry land**. O **come**, let us **worship** and **bow down**: let us **kneel** before the LORD our **maker**. For **he is our God**; and we are the **people** of his **pasture**, and the **sheep** of his hand. To day if ye will hear his **voice, harden** not your **heart**, as in the **provocation**, and as in the day of **temptation** in the **wilderness**: When your **fathers tempted** me, **proved** me, and **saw my work**.

```
T H D R Y L A N D G A I N S E
P S P I H S R O W R B A W M L
M S D N A H D I G E O S O A A
S H E E P Y E T N A V C D K P
S N E C P T V A I T E O W E M
A S O I A K O C K G A I O R N
E I W I S L R O T O L P B K E
H H A T T O P V A D L K R I D
F S K N U A U O E E E O D E R
A I O N R H T R R R W M T C A
T A F N E O N P G Y A P R I H
H E M A D E I T M O M D I O S
E S R E S T L W O E D T N V F
R T H S E E A R T H T L O A R
S L L I H S T R E N G T H D H
```

SECRET MESSAGE

_____

_____

_____

_____

_____

47

BAN LAZINESS!

Proverbs 6:6–11

Go to the ant, thou **sluggard**; **consider** her **ways**, and **be wise**: Which **having** no **guide**, **overseer**, or **ruler**, **provideth** her **meat** in the **summer**, and **gathereth** her **food** in the **harvest**. How long wilt **thou sleep**, O sluggard? when **wilt** thou **arise** out of thy sleep? Yet a little sleep, a **little slumber**, a little **folding** of the **hands** to sleep: So shall **thy poverty** come as one that **travelleth**, and thy **want** as an **armed man**.

```
F O O D F Y T R E V O P Y H T
W L H A T O O H T B E W I S E
S H I E R C L C O N S I D E R
U L H T A A P D T U T E R O F
M P U R T R O H I N S V E R B
M S M G A L M M A N K L E H S
E A T U G H E E E V G S E T E
R R C I O A H S D N I D A E N
D I L D T T R A L M R N A L P
S S T E O M E D N U A N G L T
W E I T O N O F L D M N A E N
I W O H A R V E S T S B T V S
L G A T H E R E T H I N E A T
T H E Y B I H T E D I V O R P
O V E R S E E R B L W A N T E
```

SECRET MESSAGE

_____

_____

_____

_____

_____

_____

48

TOO WONDERFUL

Proverbs 30:18–19

<u>There be</u> three things <u>which are</u> too **wonderful** <u>for</u> <u>me</u>, yea, **four** which <u>I know not</u>: **The way** of <u>an eagle</u> <u>in the air</u>; the way of a **serpent** <u>upon a rock</u>; the way of **a ship** in **the midst of the sea**; and the way of a **man with a maid**.

T H E W A Y W S E R P E N T H A
A T F O T H E E R F W I H S E
U M N O K N B A O W O E N M A
N I A S R C E R E D M U I I T
E D W N I M R T H I S W R K P
U E A K W I E N D G H R T N H
E P P A P I H S A I R I O O P
H E O C N Y T S C A E A E W N
I N T N H E E H E T H E I N R
T I E T A H A S A S C H H O A
P H T E E R E G R M G T O T F
T C H E E H O E L O A N L D T
E I R S T T A C M E E I I N T
B H O F O K O F K P R O D H V
T W O N D E R F U L E R B S T

SECRET MESSAGE

_____

_____

_____

_____

_____

_____

49

PROSPEROUS WOMAN

Proverbs 31:11–17

The **heart** of her **husband** doth **safely trust <u>in her</u>**, so that he **shall have <u>no need</u>** of **spoil**. She will do **<u>him good</u>** and **<u>not evil</u>** all the days of her life. She **seeketh wool**, and **flax**, and **worketh willingly** with her **hands**. She is like the **merchants' ships**; she **bringeth** her food from afar. She **riseth** also while it is yet **night**, and **giveth** meat to her **household**, and a **portion** to her **maidens**. She **considereth** a **field**, and **buyeth** it: with the **fruit** of her hands she **planteth** a **vineyard**. She **girdeth** her **loins** with strength, and **strengtheneth** her arms.

```
T N I G H T D N A B S U H H S
F E P M T T R L I V E T O N S
F L S E E K E T H I E N I D W
R I A C Y R F R I N O O N I O
U O F X U H C I E N L A L H O
I P E H B T T H E D H L E T L
T S L O O E T E A L I E F E A
S R Y U V G D I D N D S R K R
T P A S N N U M G R T O N R D
H O I E U I S L A R I S W O O
T R R H H R Y Y U I M G O W C
E T A O S B E S N I D G S F A
S I P L A N T E T H M E V A H
I O R D I H T E V I G A N B O
R N V V E W H S H A L L A S T
```

SECRET MESSAGE

_____

_____

_____

_____

_____

Answer Key

Puzzle 1

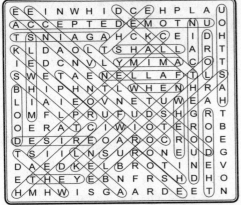

In which place did Cain live after being
driven from his garden?
Land of Nod (Genesis 4:16)

Puzzle 2

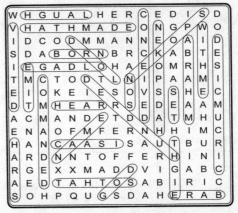

Where did God command Abraham to take
Isaac and then offer him as a burnt offering?
The land of Moriah (Genesis 22:2)

Puzzle 3

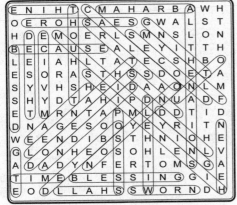

Who was the son that Abraham
did not withhold from God?
Isaac (Genesis 22:2)

Puzzle 4

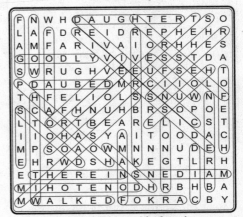

Who did Pharaoh's daughter
pay to nurse the baby?
The child's mother (Exodus 2:7–9)

Puzzle 5

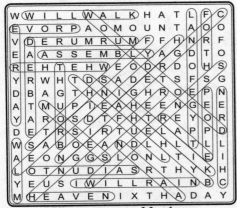

What amount of food was
gathered on the sixth day?
Twice as much (Exodus 16:5)

Puzzle 6

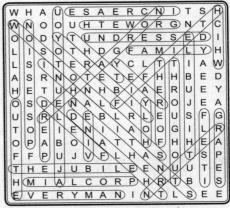

What sound declared
the Year of Jubilee?
A trumpet shall sound (Leviticus 25:9)

Puzzle 7

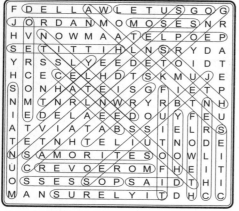

For how many days did
the men spy out the land?
Forty (Numbers 13:25)

Puzzle 8

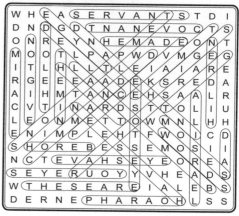

What did not wear out while
in the wilderness?
Clothes and shoes (Deuteronomy 29:5)

Puzzle 9

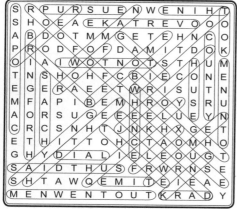

What method did the
spies use to get away?
A cord through a window (Joshua 2:15)

Puzzle 10

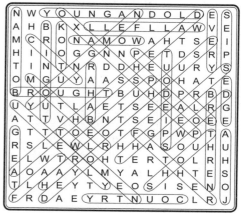

What sign did Rahab leave
to show her loyalty to Israel?
A scarlet thread (Joshua 2:21)

Puzzle 11

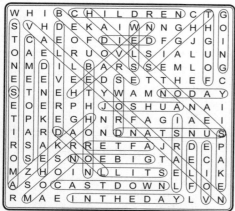

Which king of Jerusalem led
the campaign against Israel?
Adonizedec (Joshua 10:3–4)

Puzzle 12

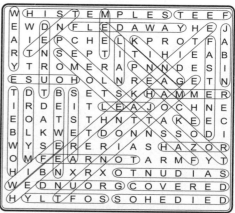

Which prophet ordered the
attack on Sisera's army?
Deborah (Judges 4:14)

Puzzle 13

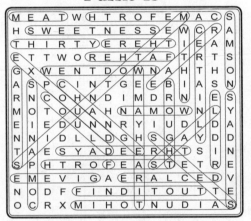

How many of Gideon's
men lapped up the water?
300 (Judges 7:7)

Puzzle 14

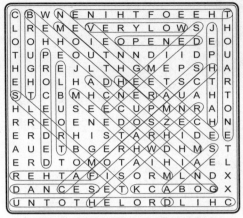

When did Jephthah surrender
his daughter to the Lord?
After two months (Judges 11:39)

Puzzle 15

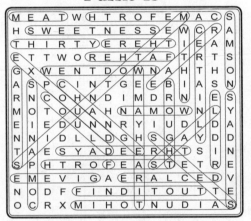

What two things did
the riddle stand for?
Honey and a lion (Judges 14:18)

Puzzle 16

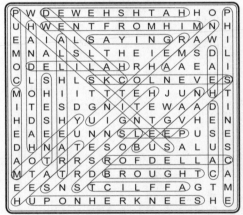

Who was the Israelite judge
with unusual strength?
Samson (Judges 16:6)

Puzzle 17

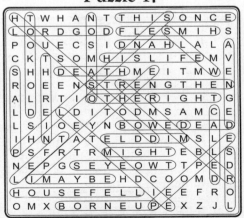

What special commitment did
Samson's strength come from?
The Nazirite vow (Judges 13:7)

Puzzle 18

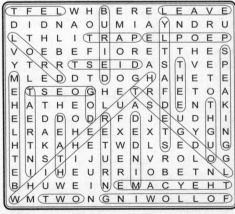

Where did Naomi and Ruth live before
they traveled together to the land of Judah?
Moab (Ruth 1:1–4)

Puzzle 19

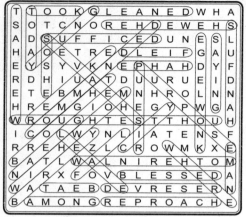

What country did
Ruth originate from?
Moab (Ruth 1:4)

Puzzle 20

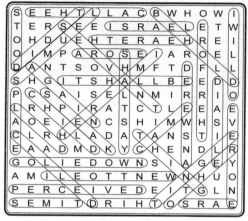

Who were the parents of this
miracle child named Samuel?
Elkanah and Hannah (1 Samuel 1:19)

Puzzle 21

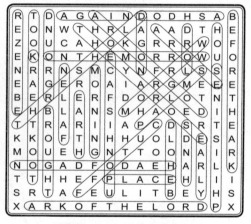

What carried the ark
home to the Israelites?
An oxen cart (1 Samuel 6:11–12)

Puzzle 22

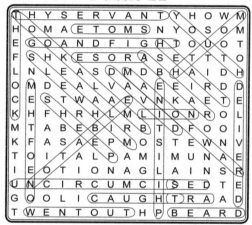

How many smooth stones did David take
from a brook as potential ammunition
against Goliath? Five (1 Samuel 17:40)

Puzzle 23

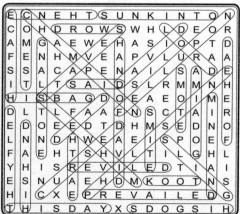

Where was the place Israel
faced the Philistines?
Shochoh (1 Samuel 17:1)

Puzzle 24

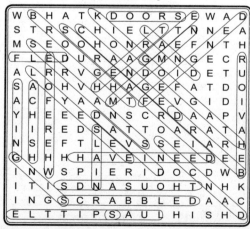

What was the name of the cave that David
escaped to after his period with King
Achish? Adullam (1 Samuel 22:1)

Puzzle 25

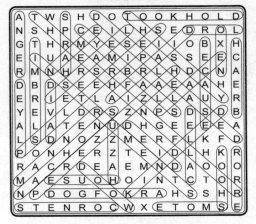

Whose house held the
ark for three months?
Obed-edom (2 Samuel 6:11)

Puzzle 26

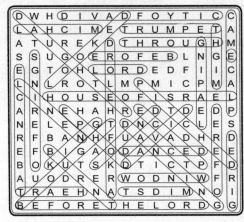

What resulted from Michal's bad attitude?
She was barren (2 Samuel 6:23)

Puzzle 27

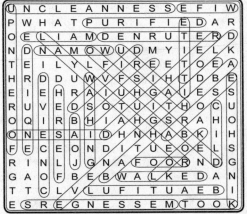

What army killed Uriah during a battle?
The Ammonites (2 Samuel 11)

Puzzle 28

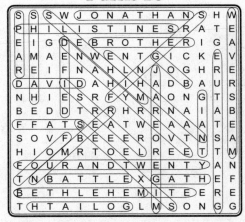

What gigantic king had an iron bed
that was over thirteen feet long?
King Og of Bashan (Deuteronomy 3:11)

Puzzle 29

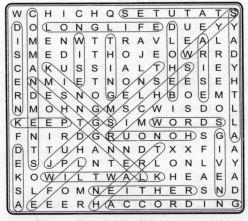

Which queen traveled to Jerusalem
to see Solomon's wisdom firsthand?
The Queen of Sheba (1 Kings 10:1)

Puzzle 30

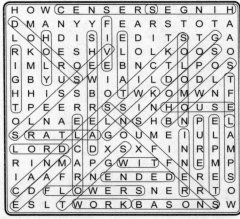

How many years total did it take Solomon
to build his own personal home?
Thirteen (1 Kings 7:1)

Puzzle 31

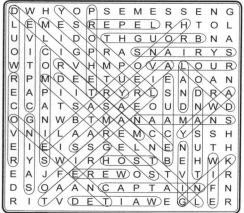

How did the queen of
Sheba test Solomon?
With hard questions (1 Kings 10:1)

Puzzle 32

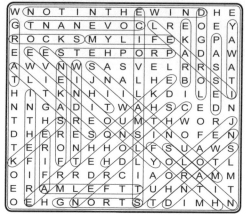

Where was Elijah hiding when
the word of the Lord came to him?
In a cave (1 Kings 19:9)

Puzzle 33

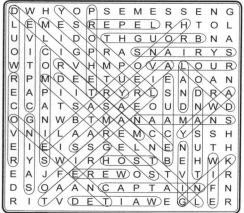

Whose messenger told Naaman
to wash in the Jordan River?
Elisha's (2 Kings 5:10)

Puzzle 34

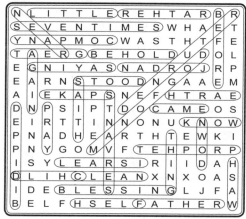

What was the leper Naaman's
position under the king of Syria?
Captain of the host (2 Kings 5:1)

Puzzle 35

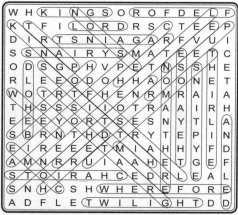

Who first discovered that
the Syrians had fled?
Four leprous men (2 Kings 7:3)

Puzzle 36

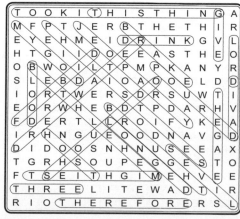

After the three mightiest, how many soldiers
were part of King David's next group of elite
warriors? Thirty (1 Chronicles 11:25)

Puzzle 37

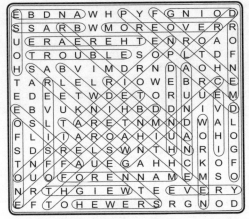

Why was David not allowed to build a
house for God? He had shed much blood
(1 Chronicles 22:8)

Puzzle 38

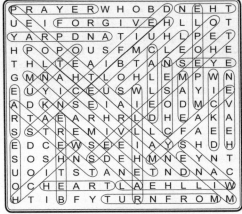

Who built the house that God
had chosen to sanctify?
Solomon (2 Chronicles 7:11)

Puzzle 39

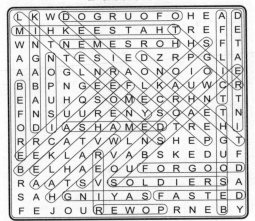

Where was Ezra going when
he asked for a safe journey?
To Jerusalem (Ezra 8:31)

Puzzle 40

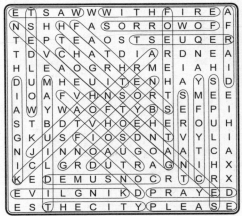

What post did Nehemiah
have with King Artaxerxes?
Cupbearer (Nehemiah 1:11)

Puzzle 41

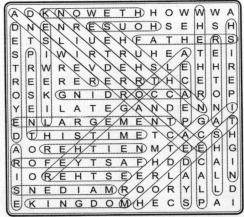

How was Esther related to Mordecai?
She was Mordecai's adopted daughter; the
daughter of Mordecai's uncle (Esther 2:7)

Puzzle 42

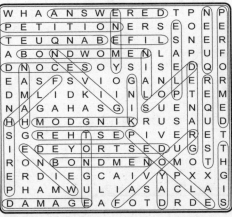

What personal possession did King
Ahasuerus give to Mordecai?
His ring (Esther 8:2)

Puzzle 43

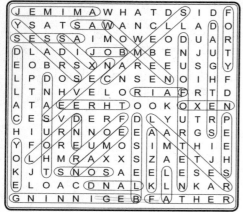

What did Satan claim would be Job's response if the Lord took everything from him? Satan claimed Job would curse God to His face (Job 1:9–11)

Puzzle 44

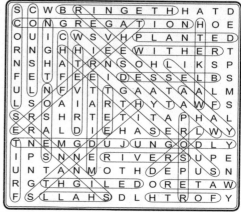

What does this psalm say shall happen to the ungodly? They shall perish (Psalm 1:6)

Puzzle 45

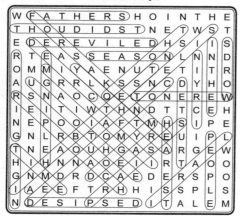

Who in the New Testament said the opening words of this psalm? Jesus (Matthew 27:46)

Puzzle 46

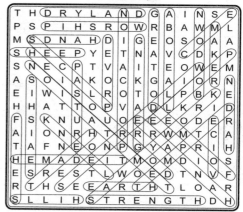

This psalm says to make what kind of noise to the Lord? A joyful noise (Psalm 95:1)

Puzzle 47

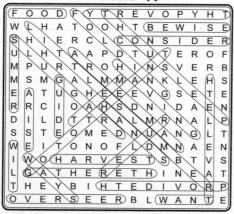

What other chapter of Proverbs makes the second and last mention of ants in the Bible? 30 (Proverbs 30:25)

Puzzle 48

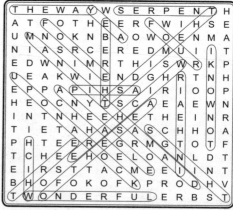

What otherwise unknown man is credited with speaking the prophecy seen in the thirtieth chapter of the Old Testament book of Proverbs? Agur (Proverbs 30:1)

Puzzle 49

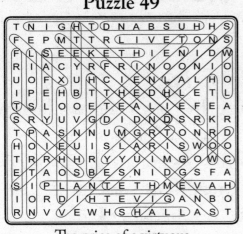

The price of a virtuous
woman is far above what?
Rubies (Proverbs 31:10)

MORE LARGE PRINT PUZZLE BOOKS!

Bible Word Searches—Large Print
Bible puzzles are a great way to pass time while learning scripture—and here's a collection of almost 50 *large print* word searches sure to satisfy the passionate Bible puzzle fan. With clues drawn from the breadth of scripture, *Bible Word Searches—Large Print* is based on the King James Version.
Paperback / 978-1-68322-170-8 / $6.99

Bible Crosswords—Large Print
Here's a collection of nearly 50 *large print* crosswords sure to satisfy the avid Bible crossword fan. With clues drawn from the breadth of scripture, *Bible Crosswords—Large Print* is based on the King James Version.
Paperback / 978-1-62416-872-7 / $5.99

Bible Crosswords—Large Print Vol. 2
If you like the first one, try volume 2! Here's a collection of dozens of *large print* crosswords sure to please the enthusiastic Bible crossword fan. With clues drawn from the breadth of scripture, *Bible Crosswords—Large Print Vol. 2* is based on the King James Version.
Paperback / 978-1-68322-169-2 / $6.99

Find These and More from Barbour
Books at Your Favorite Bookstore
www.barbourbooks.com

BARBOUR
PUBLISHING